"Steve Eggleton ... his effective use ... of John's life in God's Big Story."

Bob Hartman, author and performance storyteller

GOD
and
JOHN
Point the
WAY

Steve Eggleton

LI N
CHILDREN'S

Published by **Lion Children's**
www.lionhudson.com
Part of the SPCK Group
SPCK, 36 Causton Street,
London SW1P 4ST

ISBN 978 0 74597 949 6
eISBN 978 0 74597 950 2

First edition 2022

A catalogue record for this book is available from the British Library

Printed and bound in the United Kingdom, September 2021, LH26

Contents

CHAPTER 1

Deep Sadness

The time had come for Zechariah the priest to set off once more for his spell of duty at the Temple in Jerusalem. It was early summer, so the walk from his house in the Judaean hills would be a pleasant one.

Summer was a busy time for the farmers. There would be lots of activity in the fields and lanes, and plenty of people to talk to on the way. All this would help him to forget the ever-present sadness that lurked at the back of his mind. Sometimes it felt more like an ache in his stomach. He and his wife Elizabeth were childless.

Elizabeth had packed him a meal for the journey. He slung the bag over his shoulder and embraced her tenderly.

"God bless you, my dear," he said. "I will keep praying."

"And I will keep hoping," replied Elizabeth, as she brushed a tear away.

"Hoping and praying, what more can we do? Sometimes it feels as though God doesn't listen to our cries."

"It's all my fault, Zechariah," Elizabeth said, shaking her head. "I know that I am a disappointment to you."

Zechariah held her tightly.

"I love you more than seven sons," he said.

"But look, Zechariah. Look at my hair. It's turning grey. I'm getting too old to have children."

"At least you've got some hair, my dear," said Zechariah with a chuckle. "Look at the state of mine!"

"Please don't joke about it. I feel so ashamed. I'm afraid to walk out into the village. Everyone else has a family. Other people our age have grandchildren to hold. What will become of us, Zechariah? Who will provide for us in our old age? I am nothing more than a dried-up old tree that bears no fruit. That's the truth of the matter."

At this, Elizabeth began to sob. She lifted her apron to her face and wiped her tears. Zechariah shuffled uncomfortably.

"I must set off for my duties at the Temple in Jerusalem, but I don't like to leave you like this. Remember the barren women among our ancestors. Think of Sarah and Rachel and Hannah."

"You are right, my dear," said Elizabeth. "Today I will sing the words of the psalm 'He settles the barren woman in her home as a happy mother of children.'"

"That's my girl!" said Zechariah. "Come on. Let's set off together. You can walk with me as far as the crossroads. It will do you good to get some fresh air and exercise."

So, the two of them walked together arm in arm along the rough stony road that led from their little village in the Judaean hills towards the distant city of Jerusalem.

At the crossroads, they parted. Elizabeth walked slowly and thoughtfully back to the house, while Zechariah lengthened his stride towards the big, noisy city of Jerusalem.

Now that he was alone, it was his turn to feel gloomy. He didn't want to admit it to Elizabeth, but he was beginning to give up hope of ever having children. Elizabeth's hair was indeed turning grey. What was left of his was thin, white, and wispy, like a summer cloud on a breezy day. Zechariah was quite a bit older than his wife.

He decided that he too would cheer himself up by singing a psalm. He knew many of them by heart, but since he was on his way to Jerusalem, he chose one of the pilgrim psalms that people sang as they headed for the great city at festival times.

"I wait for the Lord, my soul waits,
and in His word, I put my hope.
My soul waits for the Lord,
More than the watchmen
Wait for the morning."

Singing these wonderful old words helped to comfort him, but deep down, Zechariah was disappointed. Since his marriage to Elizabeth, they had talked of having a family, but now they were undeniably old. They had prayed and prayed. They had taken sacrifices to the Temple, but nothing had come of it all. The years were slipping away, and it was becoming less and less likely that they would ever be able to have children.

Jerusalem was almost a day's walk from Zechariah's home in the hills, so he stopped in his usual place in the shade of a big, spreading fig tree. Here there were some flat stones set beneath the tree, smooth and polished from many years of use as seats. Zechariah liked to rest here, because there was a good view of Jerusalem in the distance. You could see its walls and towers, and on a day like this, it seemed to shine in the midday sunlight.

Zechariah took the lunch from his bag and had a long drink from the stone bottle. The water was cool and sweet. It reminded him of home. He unwrapped the square of cloth that held a small loaf of barley bread, a piece of sheep's cheese, and a lump of pressed dates. Reverently, he took the loaf and broke it in two and offered a prayer of thanks. Then, deep in thought, he slowly ate his lunch.

His eyes took in the scene around him – the fresh green leaves of early summer, and the wheat fields changing hue as they began to ripen. Then, away in the distance, the beautiful city of Jerusalem. Zechariah remembered the words of Isaiah the prophet: "I will create Jerusalem to be a delight, and its people a joy. I will rejoice over Jerusalem, and take delight in my people."

"I am getting old, Lord," Zechariah whispered. "I want to play my part in the new thing that you are doing, but I have no son. The people are becoming selfish and violent. The iron grip of the Romans seems to get ever stronger. What hope can there be for your people Israel, when the great city of Jerusalem is overrun by pagan armies?"

Zechariah looked down at the worn stone seats that were all around him, there beneath the shade of the fig tree. He thought of all the people who might have sat there over the centuries.

I wonder if our great prophet Elijah ever sat here, he thought. *Malachi, in his prophecy, says that Elijah will return. If ever we need to hear again the voice of Elijah, that time is now. Please, Almighty One, send us Elijah.*

Zechariah gathered up his things and put them into his bag. He slung it over his shoulder and picked up his stick. Then, straightening his back, he set off once more to walk the last stretch into Jerusalem.

CHAPTER 2

Scary Work for Zechariah

Late in the afternoon, Zechariah entered the bustling city of Jerusalem, with its busyness, noise, and smells. Traders called out to passers-by as everyone jostled their way through the narrow streets. Men leading pack animals with heavy loads worked their way patiently through the crowds. Many people with baskets of goods on their heads wove their way expertly to and from the traders, supplying them with fruit and vegetables, bread, and cakes for their stalls.

All this activity was fascinating for visitors, but Zechariah, who had seen it many times before, made his way steadfastly through the crowds towards the Temple. He was intent upon getting there before nightfall. Once there, he would join the rest of his team of Temple servants and priests for supper, before settling down for a good night's sleep. Then he would be ready for his fourteen days of service.

This wasn't like meeting with an ordinary bunch of workmates, or members of a sports team, because the whole group was drawn from the same family. There were fathers and sons, brothers and cousins, uncles and nephews, grandfathers and grandsons. Many of them hadn't seen one another for months, so there was a lot of catching up to be done. It was more like being at a family event. In fact, that's exactly what it was. These gatherings were a bittersweet experience for Zechariah. On the one hand, he was glad to be together with all his relatives again; on the other, it was a sad and painful reminder that he and Elizabeth had neither children nor grandchildren.

Zechariah's term of duty was two weeks long. It was always very busy. There was a constant stream of people to talk to. Many of them had brought animals or birds that had to be sacrificed in a particular way. In fact, everything in the Temple had to be done in accordance with a whole list of complicated rules that were written down in the Law. Lots of little regulations and traditions had been added over the years, so it was difficult not to make a mistake. It made Zechariah and the other attendants very nervous.

One job that was particularly scary was working with the Temple incense. This incense was a mixture of spices and resins that had to be mixed according to a special recipe. Then it had to be burnt on the golden incense altar that stood before the great embroidered curtain that screened off the Most Holy Place.

Many hundreds of years before Zechariah's time, a couple of priests – who had probably been drinking too much wine – decided that they wanted to invent a recipe of their own for the incense. They also used charcoal from somewhere other than from the big bronze altar. They were showing great disrespect for God, and they thought it was funny. God could not allow this sort of thing to go on. What would it lead to? Just as these priests were tipping out the smoking mixture onto the altar of incense, flames came out from behind the great curtain that closed off the Most Holy Place. The priests were burnt so badly that they died.

Ever since that had happened, the Temple priests had always taken great care to mix the incense exactly according to God's instructions. They were all so nervous about doing the daily task of refreshing the incense that they threw a die, to decide who would do it.

One day during his spell of duty, it fell to Zechariah to refresh the incense at the time of the evening sacrifice. Members of the public gathered as usual in the courtyard in front of the big bronze altar as the sacrifice was being made. This was a time when people could say sorry to God for the things that they had done wrong. The smell of roasting lamb drifting around them helped them to know that God forgave them, and that he would accept the sacrifice on their behalf. It was a special time of day for God's faithful people.

So, while some of his fellow priests were making the sacrifice, Zechariah went through the outer curtain and into the Holy Place. He carried with him the smoking mixture of incense and burning charcoal from the bronze altar to top up the incense on the golden altar. He knew that the new pile of burning charcoal and incense would send up a great cloud of fragrant smoke that would work its way through the outer curtain.

From the outside, the people would see the wisps of smoke curling between the curtains and drifting up into the sky. It would remind them that God was listening to their prayers. This was the place – and this was the time – for them to ask God for the things that they were longing for him to do. Many times over the years, Zechariah had watched the smoke and asked God for a family, but nothing had happened.

So now, here was Zechariah himself, standing before the altar, ready to make a new cloud of smoke. He had done this a number of times before, but still it made him nervous. He raked out the old ash and used the little bronze shovel to put it into the ash pan. He stirred the smouldering heap of incense and blew gently to get it glowing nicely. The light of the glowing embers reflected in the gold of the furniture and wall-carvings.

Then he began to add the fresh incense and charcoal, blowing gently all the while to get the fire well established. His eyes watered with the smoke. He added a little more of the mixture and watched as a new cloud of smoke rose from the little golden altar. He smiled with satisfaction at the smoke, though it made him cough.

That's a grand cloud of smoke, he thought. *It will please the people outside.*

At that very moment, a strange feeling came over him. He was no longer alone in the Holy Place. The hair stood up on the back of his neck. His heart began to thump. He could feel the sweat breaking out on his forehead.

What is going on? he thought. *Have I made a mistake with the incense? Was it wrong of me to be proud of the smoke? Am I going to be consumed by fire, like those priests long ago?*

Then he saw the angel, standing tall, just at the right-hand side of the altar. The figure was faint at first but was growing increasingly bright. The light from the seven lamps, which usually burnt so brightly from the lampstand by the wall, seemed to fade to nothing. A voice spoke, deep and clear.

"Do not be afraid, Zechariah," said the angel.

"Your prayers have been heard. Your wife Elizabeth will bear you a son..."

No, thought Zechariah. *That's just not possible.*

"... and you are to give him the name John," continued the angel. "He will be a joy and a delight to you. He will bring joy to many people because he will be great in God's sight."

Zechariah's mind was whirling.

Well, at least I'm not going to be burnt to death, he thought. Then the angel continued speaking.

"He must never take wine or fermented drink, because he will be filled with the Holy Spirit from the day he is born."

The next bit really grabbed Zechariah's attention.

"He will bring back many people to the Lord their God, and he will go on before the Lord in the spirit and power of Elijah, to turn the hearts of the fathers to their children. He will make wicked people long to be good. He will get them ready for God's promised Messiah to come."

Zechariah was immediately reminded of the words of Malachi the prophet, and the prayer that he himself had prayed only a few days before, as he sat having his lunch on the way to work. But then the old ache returned. What the angel was saying just didn't make sense. Perhaps he didn't understand that they were too old to have children. They couldn't possibly have a son. They had prayed for years and nothing had happened.

"How can an old man like me have a son?" said Zechariah. "And as for my wife Elizabeth, she is past the age when a woman can have a child."

"Don't you realize who I am?" replied the angel, becoming even brighter and more radiant than before. "I am Gabriel. I stand in the presence of God. I have been sent to speak to you, and bring you this good news."

Goodness me! thought Zechariah. *I had no idea.*

"So now," continued the angel, "because you did not believe my words, you will live in silence and not be able to speak until the child is born. What I have told you will come true at the proper time."

Zechariah wanted to apologize to the angel for not realizing who he was, but the brightness was fading, and anyway, when he opened his mouth to speak, nothing would come out.

All the time this conversation with the angel was going on, the people waiting outside in the courtyard were getting worried. What had happened to Zechariah? He was taking an awfully long time to perform his duties. Most people knew about the risk of refreshing the incense. They knew that the golden altar of incense stood right in front of the thick curtain screening off the Most Holy Place, where God's mighty awesome presence lived. Anything could happen. Perhaps Zechariah had made a mistake with the incense. Maybe he had been taken ill. If things went on much longer, someone would have to go in and pull him out.

Then, finally, the outer curtain moved and Zechariah appeared. Everybody sighed with relief. He stood on the wide steps. He looked pale. He was trembling and seemed a bit confused. Something was wrong. He held up his hand to quieten the crowd. But when he opened his mouth to speak, he couldn't say a word.

For Zechariah, this was a strange experience. He could see that the people were trying to speak to him, but he couldn't hear what they were saying. When he tried to explain what had happened to him, he could only grunt. He tried gesturing to them, but it was no use: no one could understand him.

Zechariah struggled through the remaining days of his duty at the Temple. He was glad when it was all over and he could hang up his ceremonial clothes, head off back to the hills, and return to his dear wife, Elizabeth.

CHAPTER 3

Living with a Promise

As soon as Zechariah arrived home, Elizabeth knew that something was wrong. Instead of his usual cheery call, he greeted her by banging on the door with his stick.

Supper that night was a strange experience for them both. Normally, this would be the time when Zechariah would bring Elizabeth up to date with all the family news and tell her what was going on in Jerusalem and in the wider world, but now an awkward silence filled the air.

In those days only men and boys were educated in Judaea, so Zechariah could only communicate in very basic language. Elizabeth had learned a bit from her husband, but she was not very good at either reading or writing. They found it best to have a writing tablet handy, which they used for writing a few simple words, and then, when that didn't work, they resorted to drawing pictures. However, neither of them was very good at drawing. All this was tiresome, but after a while they got used to living and communicating in this way together with lots of hand signals and funny faces.

Zechariah had tried to explain about the baby, but he could see that Elizabeth did not understand. He tried drawing on the writing tablet, but that only made things worse.

Then, after a few weeks, Elizabeth started to feel queasy, especially in the mornings. She hid this from Zechariah because she didn't want to worry him. Sometimes, she couldn't eat her food, so she would make excuses and secretly give her food to the chickens.

Then, after some months, she started to feel better, the rosiness came back to her cheeks, and she began to put on a bit of weight. She mentioned these things to the women she met at the village well each day. They smiled and looked at each other in a knowing sort of way.

One day, one of them took her aside.

"Elizabeth," she said. "I feel a bit awkward asking you this, but is it possible that you might be expecting a baby?"

Elizabeth put her hand to her mouth and her eyes grew wide.

"Really! Do you think I might be?" she asked. "I have been feeling strange lately."

"Time will tell," said her friend with a little giggle as she patted Elizabeth's tummy. Elizabeth started giggling too, and as she walked home with the jug of water, she had a job to stop smiling.

Then she remembered the strange pictures that Zechariah had tried to draw when he'd first come home from his Temple duties, unable to speak or hear.

Perhaps he's known all along, she thought.

It wasn't hard for her to get the good news across to her husband; the glow in her face and the spring in her step said it all. As her bump grew bigger, and more obvious, she was able to take her husband's hand and place it on her tummy, so that he could feel the little child moving within her.

Elizabeth decided that she wouldn't go out in public for a while. She found that she was getting rather tired, but deep down she was full of joy.

"In these days," she said, "God has shown me kindness, and taken away the disgrace of being childless."

Zechariah, too, although it was annoying being unable to hear or speak, was becoming more and more excited at the prospect of having a son. Unable to chat with his friends, he too spent a lot of time on his own. He had plenty of time to think about the words that the angel had spoken, and to pray for the little child that was growing inside Elizabeth. Would he really become the next Elijah?

Then, one day, they had a visit from a young woman from distant Nazareth.

CHAPTER 4

Another Baby on the Way

Once the baby John had been growing inside Elizabeth for six months, Gabriel, the angel who had appeared to Zechariah, appeared again. This time, he brought a very important message to a young woman who lived in Nazareth in Galilee. Her name was Mary. She was a relative of Elizabeth and she was promised in marriage to a carpenter called Joseph.

Just as Zechariah had been, Mary was scared when she saw the angel.

"Don't be afraid, Mary," he said. "You have been specially chosen by God. You will have a baby, who will grow up to be a king like David. He will be the great Messiah that God has promised."

"How can I possibly have a baby?" asked Mary. "I don't yet have a husband."

"The Holy Spirit will come upon you, and God's power will overshadow you. You will miraculously become pregnant. The child will be called Jesus. He will be God's Son."

Then Gabriel told Mary about Elizabeth.

"Your relative Elizabeth, even though she is getting old, is going to have a baby," said the angel. "She is already six months pregnant."

Gabriel knew that this was news to Mary. He stood silently for a while to let his words sink in, then he said, "With our God, nothing is impossible."

This news about Elizabeth was a great encouragement to Mary. She knew that Elizabeth had been asking God for a child for many years, and that now she was far too old to be a mother. If God could give Elizabeth a child, Mary reasoned, then he could work a miracle in her too, and she could trust him to deal with all the questions that were beginning to whirl around in her mind.

These comforting thoughts enabled her to look directly at the strange and awesome presence that was bringing her this message and speak with quiet confidence.

"Yes, I will do it. Let it be done to me just as you have said."

As soon as the angel had gone, Mary knew what she had to do. First, she must get a message to Joseph, and then she urgently wanted to visit Elizabeth. She knew that they would be able to talk about what was happening, and that Elizabeth would understand.

Mary sent a message to Zechariah and Elizabeth by some passing merchants, to let them know that she would visit them just as soon as she could. Then she began to look for an opportunity to go.

It would take about four days to walk from Nazareth in Galilee to the Judaean hills, where Zechariah and Elizabeth lived. A young woman of Mary's age would never dream of making a journey like that on her own. She would have to wait until some of the men from her family were going that way.

Mary was impatient to set off as soon as she could, so when she heard that her cousin and two of her uncles were planning to take some cattle up to Jerusalem, she asked if she could go with them.

CHAPTER 5

John Meets Jesus

As the baby John grew inside her, Elizabeth was taking time to be still and quiet. Zechariah, too, was spending a lot of time alone, thinking, praying, and reading the Scriptures. Both of them were praying daily for the child, and asking for wisdom to know how best to bring him up to be exactly what God wanted him to be.

Then, early one afternoon, Mary arrived, accompanied by her cousin. Elizabeth had noticed that her own little baby had been getting restless throughout the day, but when she heard the latch on the door, and Mary's voice calling a greeting, the baby started wriggling and jumping vigorously.

Elizabeth went to the door with her hand on her tummy to quieten the babe. She felt a warm tingling all over, as God's Holy Spirit came upon her. The two women embraced warmly. They stood holding each other, tears rolling down their cheeks. It was such a relief to be together. They had both been chosen to play an important part in the great events that were taking place around them.

Elizabeth held Mary at arms' length and started speaking. The words were clear and deliberate, and seemed to come from deep within her. She was looking straight at Mary.

"Blessed are you among women, Mary," she said, "and blessed is the child that you will bear."

Elizabeth held Mary close. Inside her, the little child John could sense the closeness of the tiny body of Jesus as his mother hugged Mary. He was overwhelmed with silent joy. Elizabeth felt her growing baby buzzing with excitement within her.

"Why am I so special that you should come here to visit me?" she said to Mary. "To think that you will be the mother of my Lord."

The two women looked at each other and smiled through their tears.

"As soon as I heard your call," said Elizabeth, "little John went crazy. He was jumping and wriggling with delight."

Elizabeth spoke her words deliberately, gently squeezing Mary's hand with every word.

"Mary, you are so blessed! You have believed that what God has said will come true."

Then it was Mary's turn to speak. As soon as she heard her, Elizabeth could tell that these were no ordinary words. They sounded like a poem that came from her heart, strong and confident:

"My soul glorifies the Lord.
My spirit is full of joy to the God who saved me.
He has chosen just an ordinary girl,
And now for years to come,
People will call me 'blessed'.
For God the Mighty One has done amazing
*   things.*
His Name is holy.
He is full of mercy to those who respect Him,
To their children and grandchildren too.
He has worked powerful miracles,
And swept away those who think they are
*   great.*
He has knocked the proud off their perch,
And promoted ordinary people.
He has given food to the hungry,
But sent the rich away with nothing.
He has kept his promise to his people Israel,
Just as he promised to Abraham
And all his children
Down through the ages."

All this time, the young man who had accompanied Mary looked on in amazement as he watched these two women and heard what they had to say. He saw his cousin in a new light.

Then, all of a sudden, Elizabeth noticed him. She had been so excited at Mary's visit that she had completely ignored him.

"I'm so sorry," she said. "I have completely neglected to welcome you."

"No," said the young man. "I understand, but I need to get back to Jerusalem."

Elizabeth insisted that she should pack up a few things for his journey. He stood and waited as she wrapped some bread and cheese in a cloth, and topped up his water bottle. He put these things in his bag, and then set off back to Jerusalem. He knew that he wouldn't get there before nightfall, but anyway, he needed time to think, after all that he had seen and heard.

Mary stayed with Elizabeth and Zechariah for three months until Elizabeth's baby was due to be born. These were wonderful days for both women. They did a lot of talking together, and they prayed for the children that they were carrying. They were able to encourage one another. Each of them faced difficult times ahead. Mary was also able to help with things around the house as Elizabeth got bigger and less able to move about easily.

It seemed to Elizabeth that John continued to wriggle and kick inside her so much more while Mary was with her.

"Perhaps he is impatient to start his work," she said to Mary. "I'm sure he knows that you are carrying the Redeemer of Israel."

As the time came near for Elizabeth to have her baby, Zechariah and Elizabeth arranged for Mary to be accompanied back to Nazareth to Joseph the carpenter, who was soon to be her husband.

Meanwhile, back in the hill country of Judaea, the last weeks of Elizabeth's pregnancy passed by until the day came when John was born. Zechariah and Elizabeth were so delighted to be able to hold their very own son in their arms. Whenever he cried too much, Elizabeth would simply give him to Zechariah to hold, because Zechariah couldn't hear a thing.

CHAPTER 6

God is Gracious

When everybody in the village and the surrounding hill country heard what God had done for Zechariah and Elizabeth, they were amazed and very excited.

Eight days after the birth, lots of friends and relations gathered at Zechariah and Elizabeth's house for the naming ceremony. The priest arrived to perform the circumcision. He knew Zechariah and his family well. He laid out his equipment and washed his hands. Then he took the baby from Elizabeth.

"So, what's to be this little fellow's name?" he asked. "I'm assuming it will be Zechariah."

"Oh no," answered Elizabeth. "No, not Zechariah. He is to be called John."

"You can't be serious, Elizabeth," said the priest, looking at her anxiously. "You don't have any relatives with that name."

A murmur went around the room. Everybody was in agreement. He really should be called Zechariah, especially as he would be the only son that Zechariah and Elizabeth were likely to have. This was their only chance to keep the family name alive. Perhaps Elizabeth was playing some sort of trick on Zechariah while he couldn't hear what was going on.

Elizabeth looked round at all her friends and family.

"Ask his father," she said defiantly. "Ask Zechariah. He will tell you what the child is to be called. Where's our writing tablet?"

Somebody passed the writing slate and the chalk to the priest. He wrote a message on it and passed it to Zechariah. Everyone was making signs to him, so he knew what all the fuss was about.

Zechariah took the slate. He wiped it clean with his sleeve and glanced at Elizabeth. They exchanged a knowing little smile. Slowly he began to write. He was enjoying this. Everybody crowded around to watch.

"His name is to be..." The priest stood holding the baby. He was watching Zechariah intently, fully expecting that the next word would be "Zechariah", but the chalk slowly spelled out in large letters "J-O-H-N."

Immediately the room erupted in noisy chatter. Shocked and surprised, everybody was speaking at once. The priest looked a bit troubled.

There was so much commotion in the room that nobody noticed the miracle at first. Zechariah was speaking again.

Gradually, all the friends and relations realized what was going on. One by one, they stopped talking and looked at Zechariah. His face beamed with joy. He was looking up with his hands raised towards heaven. His eyes were closed. He spoke loudly and clearly as though he was standing in the synagogue reading from a scroll.

"Praise the Lord, the God of Israel, who has come and brought salvation to his people." Zechariah continued to speak wonderful words of praise and worship to God. Then he took the little baby from the priest and cradled him in his arms. Looking down at the child, he spoke directly to him, his voice low and strong.

"And you, my child, will be called a prophet of the Most High God. You will go before the Lord to prepare the way for him."

All the friends and relations stood in silence, looking at the miracle of this little child in his father's arms, and listening to these wonderful, strong, clear words from Zechariah, who had been living in silence for the past nine months. He continued his speech to John.

"You will speak words that will bring people to salvation through the forgiveness of their sins, because of the tender mercy of our God, by whom the Rising Sun will come to us from heaven, to shine on the people who are living in darkness, and who are afraid of death, to guide our feet into the path of peace."

As soon as Zechariah had finished these words, everyone clapped and thanked God for the miracles that they had seen and heard.

Zechariah handed the baby back to the priest, who completed the naming ceremony. Everyone cheered and clapped when it was announced that his name would be John. They all knew that it meant "God is Gracious". They realized that something new was beginning.

News of these amazing events soon spread throughout the Judaean hill country, filling people with hope. Things were beginning to move in the right direction at last.

"What will this child become?" they asked one another.

"John, eh? Well, I never!"

"God is Gracious."

"Yes, indeed."

CHAPTER 7

Escape to the Desert

The first months of John's life as a little baby were truly wonderful. Zechariah and Elizabeth were so happy to be parents. This was what they had always dreamed of. They were full of thankfulness to God for answering their prayers.

Zechariah had to be at the Temple for all the pilgrim feasts as well as for his annual fourteen days of duty. In this way he was able to keep up with news from the wider world. Elizabeth and Zechariah had heard from Mary and Joseph that their son, Jesus, had been born in Bethlehem. All was well.

Then came news that troubled the people of Jerusalem. A group of important men had arrived from distant lands far away to the east. They had been studying the stars and all sorts of ancient writings, and they had decided that there must be a new king born somewhere in Judaea.

This kind of thing was likely to cause trouble. The Romans were in control of all the lands around the Mediterranean Sea, but their empire didn't go very much further east. Herod was king of Judaea, but he had to do what he was told by the Romans, or he would be in trouble. He was trying to keep both the Jewish people and the Romans happy. A nasty, cruel man, he actually kept very few people happy.

When these important men arrived from a distant land, Herod became very worried and tried to find out where this new king was supposed to be born. He had spies everywhere.

One morning, there came a loud and urgent knocking at the door of Zechariah and Elizabeth's house. Zechariah stood on a stool and peered out of the high window that was near the door. He sensed that something was wrong.

"Who's there?" he asked in a loud whisper.

"I have an urgent message for you from Joseph of Nazareth. Can I come in?"

"Wait a moment," said Zechariah, jumping down from the stool. He went to the door and let the young man in.

"You look exhausted," said Zechariah. "Let me fetch you some water. Please, take a seat."

"Thank you," said the visitor. "I came in haste." He slumped into a chair, and Zechariah brought him a jug of water and a cup. He drank the first cupful in one go, then he poured himself another. The man spoke in short bursts between sips of water.

"Joseph Ben Jacob. Carpenter from Nazareth. He and his wife had a visit. Delegation from some distant country away to the east. Wealthy men, and God-fearing. They called on Herod first. That was a mistake. He told them to return with news of the child's whereabouts." He paused to catch his breath and then continued.

"They thought it best not to return to Herod, but he will soon find out where they have been. Meanwhile, he will be sending his men to scour the area for young boys. God spoke to Joseph in a dream. Told him to escape. Take his family away. He's gone, but he didn't tell anybody where. Very wise. Asked me to get a message to you. Soon as possible. Worried about your little boy. 'Take him away,' he said, 'before it's too late. Take him somewhere safe.'"

"We had heard about the men from the East," said Zechariah. "They came to Jerusalem to visit Herod. They caused quite a stir."

"Of course," said the man. "They were important men. A big group, what with servants and security people and the like. You can be sure that Herod will be upset. Who knows what he will do?"

"I will speak to my wife. We have friends down in the desert."

"Go there as soon as you can," said the messenger urgently. "Don't wait. Just go. Herod has spies everywhere."

Zechariah went to find Elizabeth. He told her what the young man had said.

"I am not surprised, Zechariah," she said calmly. "We must expect this sort of thing. I will get ready straight away."

They thanked the messenger and sent him off with some water and some cakes for his journey.

"Don't worry," he said as he left. "I will take another route back. We don't want Herod's spies to know where I have been. God bless you all, and may his angels watch over you." With that, their visitor slipped out and was gone.

"Now Elizabeth," said Zechariah, "I think we ought to take this seriously. God has trusted us with this little fellow. We must do our utmost to keep him from harm."

"We will need to wait for sundown, so nobody knows where we have gone," said Elizabeth.

"That's good. Yes, once it's dark, you can take the small water jar to the well. You can take little John with you. It will just look like a last-minute top up. No one will think it strange." Zechariah was beginning to warm to the idea of a night-time adventure.

"I will bring the things we need," Zechariah continued. "Let's meet where the track goes off into the wilderness. There should be a good moon tonight. We will find our way easily enough. The Essene brothers at the monastery will give us shelter."

So that evening, as the light faded, Elizabeth took the small water jar. She slung a light bag of things over her shoulder, and taking little John by the hand, she set off for the well. It had only been a matter of weeks since John had learned to walk, so progress was rather slow.

Zechariah gave her some time to get ahead of him, then he slipped a note into the house next door.

> *Have been called away. Will be in touch.*
> *Please water the plants and feed the*
> *chickens as usual, Zechariah.*

He left the house quietly, carrying a large bag over his shoulder. He was hoping and praying that he wouldn't meet anybody. Thankfully, all was quiet in the village.

The little family met in the moonlight as planned, and then set off towards the Judaean desert and the Dead Sea. With John needing to be carried much of the way, it was going to be a long journey. They knew that it would not be possible to get all the way to the monastery in one night, so as soon as the sun began to rise, they found a shady place close to some rocks and overshadowed by thorn bushes. There they settled down to rest. When the sun began to go down again, they set off once more to walk through another moonlit night.

The following morning, they arrived at the monastery. Zechariah knew the brothers well. Some of them worked alongside him as priests at the Temple in Jerusalem. They were a warm and friendly bunch.

"Come on in, and welcome," said the brother who opened the door. "You look tired. I will get you something to eat."

The brothers took them to the refectory and brought them warm fresh bread, a little cheese, and some dates. Zechariah and Elizabeth explained about the message from Joseph.

"You can stay here as long as you like," said Brother Levi, who was in charge of housekeeping. "I will find you a room."

So, before the end of that first day, they had a little room in which to live. It was very plain, but it was clean, and there was food and water.

They joined the brothers for their daily meals at midday, then again in the evening. These took place in the refectory. The brothers came in wearing white gowns, which they put on after their special bath. They spoke quietly and politely to each other.

Little John, although he was very young, watched all the goings on at the monastery over the months that the family stayed there. He saw how friendly and gentle the brothers were with each other, and with his parents. He liked it there. He felt at home. He felt secure.

The monastery was not so very far from Jerusalem – not much further than Zechariah and Elizabeth's home in the Judaean hills was from the big city. It was a walk that could be done in a day. The only real difference was that from the monastery, the road was much drier and dustier. Nobody would dream of making such a journey without plenty of water in their bag.

So, Zechariah was able to continue his work at the Temple as though nothing had happened. He decided that he wouldn't tell anyone where they were living, just to be on the safe side.

As soon as Zechariah arrived in Jerusalem for his next tour of duty, he was shocked to hear about the terrible things that had been going on while he and his family had been at the monastery. King Herod had heard, from the men who had arrived from the East, that a king had been born somewhere in the area. They had failed to return with news of exactly where the child was. So, in his rage, Herod had sent his troops to slaughter all the young boys in Bethlehem and all the villages that surrounded Jerusalem. Some of Zechariah's relatives had lost their sons in this way.

Zechariah was so thankful that little John was safe, but he felt deeply sad to think of all those families who were missing their young boys. He thought of all the mothers who were weeping every day with grief. He remembered the words of the prophet Jeremiah:

"A voice is heard in Ramah,
Mourning and great weeping.
Rachel weeping for her children

And refusing to be comforted
Because her children are no more."

CHAPTER 8

The Boy John

As John grew older and learned how to speak, he understood more of what was going on around him. Zechariah talked to him about God. John loved to sit on his father's knee and hear all the exciting stories from the ancient Hebrew Scriptures.

But there was another story that little John asked for again and again. It was the story of how the angel appeared to Zechariah in the Temple and told him that he and Elizabeth were going to have a baby boy.

"What did the angel say his name should be?" John asked every time he heard the story. Then Zechariah would tease him.

"Well," said Zechariah. "I can't remember exactly. Let me think. Was it Joseph, I wonder?"

"No," said John. "It wasn't Joseph."

"Aha! Now I remember," said Zechariah, a glint in his eye. "It was to be Moses."

"No, no, no, it was John. It was John, John, John!"

"Really?" replied Zechariah. "And there was me thinking it was Jacob. My poor old memory. It's not so good these days."

"Abba, the angel really did say John, didn't he?" asked John earnestly.

Then Zechariah would hold his little boy tightly and let out a deep, warm chuckle.

"Yes, of course it was John, but I was getting old and grey, and so was your mother. To my shame, I didn't believe that God could give us a little boy and so I lost my power of speech and my hearing too. It was like being shut in a silent room. I had plenty of time to think and pray, and who do you think I was praying for most of all? I will tell you. I prayed for my little boy John, who was going to come like the great prophet Elijah and teach the people how to behave properly. My little John was going to prepare the way for God's promised Messiah.

"These are exciting times, my boy, and you are going to play an important part in the history of your people."

"Tell me about baby John, Abba," said John, twirling a lock of old Zechariah's beard with his finger.

"Even before you were born, you were prophesying. You had been growing inside your mother for just six months – that's half a year – when we had a special visitor. Mary came to visit us. Inside her, but still very tiny, was Jesus, the promised Messiah. You were only this big." Zechariah held his hands apart to show John his size. John matched his little hands to his father's big, wrinkled ones and thoughtfully considered the measurement.

"Was I really only this big?" he asked.

"You were, my brave boy, but you were big enough to know that God's Chosen One was in the house, and he was only this big." Here Zechariah indicated the size between a finger and thumb. Once again, John matched the size with his own hand and considered it.

"You jumped and wriggled enough to make your mother wonder what was going on. She cried out in surprise.

"You can imagine how excited we were when you were born. We had prayed and waited for you for so many years. At last God had answered our prayers, but the real excitement came when you were eight days old, and everybody gathered in the house for the naming ceremony. What a day!

"There were relatives and friends all crowded into the house. The priest took you in his arms and then asked your mother what your name should be. I was just looking on. I couldn't hear a word, but I knew what they were saying. When your mother said that your name was to be John, everyone looked shocked, especially the priest. You should have seen their faces! He asked her again, so she told him to ask me.

They brought me a writing slate and tried to explain what they wanted, but they didn't need to explain. I knew what they were after. I had been looking forward to this moment. I wrote very slowly. Everybody crowded round to watch, expecting me to write 'Zechariah' or something, but I wrote 'His – name – is – to – be...' and then I waited. I could see that they were getting agitated, but remember, I couldn't hear a thing.

"Then I slowly spelled out your name. 'J-O-H-N' – John."

At this Zechariah laughed, and the little boy on his knee clapped his hands with delight.

"Hooray!" cried little John. "I knew his name would be John."

"I had no sooner written the name," continued Zechariah, "when a great noise burst upon my ears. Suddenly I could hear again. Everyone in the room was talking excitedly. They all felt that something remarkable was happening. Then I found myself singing and praising God. I could speak again!

"Gradually the people in the room realized that I was speaking, so they quietened down to listen. I felt God giving me some special words, firstly for him, and then for you – that you were going to be a prophet of the Most High God, getting people ready to meet the Chosen One who God would send. You were going to show people where they were going wrong, and help them to turn around and do what is right.

"That's what you are, little John. You are a prophet. God is going to use you to prepare the way for his promised Messiah to come."

The other stories that John liked to hear were the ones about the prophet Elijah. He knew that he was going to have to do a similar job, so again and again he asked his father to tell him the story of how Elijah had bravely stood up to the wicked king Ahab. He and his nasty queen, Jezebel, had arranged for a nearby farmer called Naboth to be killed, so that they could have his vineyard. Elijah had not been afraid to tell them that they were wrong to kill Naboth and steal his vineyard. He had also shown them plainly that God was real and true, and very strong. Perhaps the story that John liked to hear most was how God had fed Elijah when he was hungry, and had comforted him when he was troubled and lonely.

As he grew older, John realized that his task was not going to be an easy one. He wondered whether, like Elijah, he might one day have to deal with a cruel king or a corrupt Roman governor.

CHAPTER 9

Bigger and Bushier

From the start, Zechariah and Elizabeth knew that John was going to be a holy man, with a special job to do for God. He was to be a Nazirite, which meant that he must never drink anything with alcohol in it, like wine or beer. The other thing was that his hair was allowed to grow long.

When he was a little boy, nobody really noticed he was different, but as he grew bigger, it became more and more obvious.

It was fashionable for Roman men to cut their hair short, and to shave their beards every day. John's hair and beard were naturally curly, so as the years passed, they just got bushier and bushier. It made him look rather wild. He stood out from the more fashionable people.

The first time that John and his parents were at the monastery, he had been very young, so he didn't remember much, except that the brothers were very kind to them. As he became older, he visited them again and again. He learned a great deal from the way they lived their lives. They wanted to please God with everything they did, including what they thought.

Although the monastery was in a hot, dry, and dusty place, there were special pipes to bring water from the nearby mountains, so that not only was there enough water for drinking and washing, but there was enough to fill a large pool. It had steps going down into it, but it was not designed for swimming. It was for washing; not just for getting rid of the sweat and dirt, it had a more important job to do.

Every day, once the brothers had finished their work, they went to the pool and walked down the steps into the water. Then they came up the steps on the other side. They did this carefully and thoughtfully, because they wanted God to make them clean, not just from ordinary dirt, but from the wrong things that they had said and done and thought.

After they had been in the pool, they would dry themselves, then put on a clean white gown before going into the refectory for their evening meal. This daily habit of going through the pool before supper made a big impression upon John.

As he got older, he realized how helpful it was for that community of brothers. They were very friendly and hospitable people, and had lots of fun together, but they were always careful to be gentle and courteous. John understood that if you are going to live together happily as brothers and sisters in God's family, you need to have a good way of dealing with mistakes. You can't afford to hold on to any kind of grudge or resentment.

So, although John didn't actually join the brothers and become a full member of the community at the monastery, he learned some important lessons there. He was always welcomed as a friend and he enjoyed helping the brothers with their daily work.

Having such good friends at the monastery was particularly helpful some years later, after his father Zechariah and his mother Elizabeth had died. He spent most of his time in the desert, and he learned to survive on the wild foods that he could find there, but at the monastery he was able to use the library. He studied the Hebrew Scriptures and learned about God and the history of his people. John knew that he had a special job to do for God. He knew that it was important for him to know and understand the Scriptures. He wanted to learn as much as he could. He needed to know for sure how God wanted him to live, and what he wanted him to say.

John might have looked a bit wild and scary, but as he grew bigger and bushier, he was also growing wiser and becoming more gentle and more gracious inside. He was a very special man. During this time in the Judaean desert, God was preparing him for the important task ahead.

CHAPTER 10

The Jordan

The years went by, and John waited. He knew that he was going to be preaching publicly. He knew that he was going to use water, as the brothers did, to help people understand about right and wrong. God had showed him this much, but he felt that there was more he needed to know.

One day, as John sat in the monastery library reading the writings of the great prophet Isaiah, he began to understand something very important that few people at the time had realized. God's chosen Messiah was going to have to die, to pay for all the bad and evil things in the world.

As a boy, John had often been at the Temple in Jerusalem. When his father Zechariah offered the morning or evening sacrifice, he had joined the crowds and watched the smoke rising up into the sky. He had heard the people around him praying and asking God to forgive them for the things they had done, the air thick with the fragrance of roasting lamb. He knew that for many of his fellow Jews, the smell of roast lamb was the smell of God's forgiveness.

"He was pierced for the evil things that we had done." The words of Isaiah's prophecy were shocking. "It was because of our sins that he was wounded. He was beaten for the evil that we had done. He was arrested, and sentenced, and led off to die, slaughtered like a lamb."

As he read on, John began to understand that God's chosen Servant was going to have to suffer, and like those lambs that were offered in the Temple, he too was going to have to be sacrificed.

Goodness me, he thought, as he read Isaiah's words. *If my father was right, and our kinsman Jesus really is God's Chosen One, he is going to have a very tough job to do. Perhaps I should call him "God's Lamb".*

John also made a point of reading about the prophet Elijah. These were the stories that his father had told him when he was small. He knew that in some way he himself would need to be bold and brave like Elijah.

As he read the story of Elijah standing up to King Ahab again, John bowed his head.

"Give me the strength, Lord," he prayed, "to be as brave as Elijah was."

All this was preparing him for the day when he would stand by the Jordan river and talk to people about the coming Messiah.

Then, one morning, John felt God's Holy Spirit stirring him. It was as though someone was winding him up, filling him with a restless energy. He felt God saying, "It is time to leave this place and go. Walk northwards up the Jordan river until you find the right spot."

So, early the next morning, John gathered a few things into a bag and slung it over his shoulder. He said goodbye to the brothers at the monastery. A group of them stood around him and spoke a blessing over him. These were words they knew well. They all spoke them together.

"May the Lord bless you and keep you. May the Lord make his face to shine upon you. May the Lord lift up the light of his countenance upon you and give you peace."

John stood with his head bowed. It was blessing enough to hear the brothers praying together like this, and it was good to know that they were there at the northern end of the Dead Sea. It wasn't too far away from where he would be preaching. He knew that there would always be a welcome for him at the monastery.

So, John went on a search for the right place to start his public work. He knew that God had chosen him to do this special job. He didn't want to get it wrong.

It was a beautiful clear morning when he set out. The first few miles of his journey took him along the shores of the salty Dead Sea. Then he swung northwards to follow the banks of the winding Jordan river, looking for a good place to make a start on the work that God had called him to do.

As he journeyed along, he began to think of all the amazing things that God had done in and around the Jordan. He prayed that he would be as faithful to God as so many of those who had gone before him.

There was Joshua, the great military leader. He was strong and brave, and after Moses died, he led the people of Israel across this Jordan river and into the land of promise.

He thought of the young prophet Elisha. When God carried the old prophet Elijah away up into heaven at the end of his life, Elisha took up Elijah's old coat and struck the waters of the Jordan with it. God made the waters part, so that he could walk across and become the new prophet instead of Elijah. It was comforting for John to think of Elisha starting his career as a prophet here at the Jordan.

Then he remembered Naaman. He was commander of the Syrian army. He was a proud and important man, but he had the dreaded disease of leprosy. He visited Elisha, but when Elisha sent him to wash in the Jordan river, he refused, because it wasn't respectable enough for him.

Then John remembered that it was Naaman's servant who had persuaded his master to do as

Elisha had told him and wash in the Jordan river. Naaman listened to his servant. He washed seven times in the river, and he was healed.

That's it, thought John. *I am like that servant. I will call the people of this nation, whoever they are, to wash in this old river. Just like Naaman, we all have a disease. We all suffer from this sickness of our souls, this rebellion, this selfishness and disobedience.*

As he continued to stride out, he turned his thoughts to prayer.

"Your Son Jesus has come, Lord," he prayed. "I know that one day he will become a sacrifice, to put us right with you, Lord. I know we need to own up to the things that we have done wrong. We have all gone our own way, just like sheep without a shepherd. That's what the prophet Isaiah said."

As John walked along, he was getting more and more excited. He felt that things were beginning to fall into place. He was understanding more clearly what God was wanting him to do.

It was getting towards nightfall, when John at last arrived at a spot where the river widened out. It was a place where animals and carts could cross in the shallower water. At this time of day, there were still a few people about, but it was easy to see, from the size of the track that ran westwards from the river, that this was a busy crossing place.

"This is where I shall make a start," he said to himself. "But for now, I will find somewhere to sleep."

The next day, John arrived at the river early in the morning. People were already coming and going. He stood and watched as oxcarts loaded with fruit and vegetables trundled into the water up to their axles. People crossing on foot, with baskets on their heads, waded through the water with their robes gathered up in their arms to keep them dry; others hitched lifts on the passing carts to keep their sandals dry, or held on to the carts to steady themselves.

John was fascinated. As a child, he had visited the crowded city with his parents, but as an adult, much of his time had been spent alone. He wasn't really used to being with lots of people. Here, as he stood and watched them, John felt God's Spirit coming upon him, filling him with love for all these people.

"I need to speak to them, Lord," he prayed. "I must begin the work. I must tell them to get ready for your Promised One. He will soon be here. I know he will, but how do I begin? I am not really sure."

John went down to the water's edge. He kicked off his sandals and waded into the deeper water. People could see that he was some sort of holy man with his rough camel-hair coat and leather belt, and his long hair and beard.

Then one of the cart drivers recognized him.

"Hey, it's John, son of Zechariah. What brings you here, young man?" This was just what he needed to get him started.

"I am here to prepare people for the Lord's Messiah." John was simply replying to the man's greeting, but as he stood in the water amid all the people coming and going, he continued with more volume, so that more people could hear him.

"God's Promised One is coming. He will soon be with us. We must all get ready to meet him. Let's turn away from all the evil that we have done. Let's speak it out and wash in this Jordan river, to show that we mean it. Let's make up our minds that we want to start a new chapter and prepare our hearts to meet him."

Everybody stopped to listen. John looked from one to another.

"Come on then. Come down into the water. Speak out the evil. Wash it away. Turn around and live the sort of life that pleases God."

One by one, the people began to come to him. He led them into deeper water, and there he encouraged them to speak out the things that were troubling their consciences. He laid them down until the water closed over them, and then he helped them back onto their feet. John's work had begun.

"I am baptizing you with water, but the one who is coming after me is much greater than I am. He will baptize you with the Holy Spirit and with fire."

It continued like this all that first day. People kept coming and asking what was going on. So John had to keep explaining, and then baptizing.

The next day, more people came. As the days went by, the people were not just those who happened to be passing through. They were coming out from Jerusalem and all the surrounding towns and villages to hear this holy man preaching.

Before long, hundreds of people were coming to hear John and see the baptisms. Some came down to John in the water. Others just watched. John could see how some people were eager to speak out their sins and be baptized. Many of them wept and asked God to forgive them, but there were some who stood at a distance with arms folded and grim faces. They would not come down into the river.

As the days and weeks and months went by, more and more people came. Even some of the fishermen from Galilee came to hear John's preaching and be baptized. Some of them joined a little team of those who helped John in this special work.

All sorts of people came to the Jordan to hear John. The people that collected taxes for the Romans came and asked him what they should do.

"It's quite simple," answered John. "Don't collect any more money than you should." A murmur went around the crowd as, one after another, these men went down into the water to be baptized by John.

Some of the Roman soldiers came to see what was going on. They stood in a group on the bank.

"What are we supposed to do then, John?" one of the soldiers called out. Everyone stood in silence, wondering how John would answer him.

"Don't use your position to get money out of people," answered John, "and don't accuse anyone falsely. Oh, and by the way," added John with a little smile and wag of his finger, "be content with your wages."

One of the young soldiers took off his helmet. He unstrapped his breastplate and belt with its sword.

"Here, hold this a minute," he said to one of his fellow soldiers, dumping the gear into his arms. Bravely, he walked down to John in the water.

There was a brief conversation with John, after which the soldier was taken down under the water. All those who were watching clapped as he came up dripping from the river and took back the kit from his friend. Then another soldier did the same. Then another, and another. The people were amazed, but they feared for John, that this would get him into trouble.

"I am baptizing you with water," said John, eyeing the crowds. "But one more powerful than I will come. I am not worthy even to unbuckle his sandals. He will baptize you with the Holy Spirit and fire."

One day, a big crowd came down to the river from Jerusalem. Among them were some of the religious leaders. They had come to see what all the fuss was about. They stood together along the banks of the river with faces like stone.

"Well now," said John, looking up at them staring grimly down at him. "Here's a fine nest of poisonous snakes. Who invited you? Do you really want to turn away from your evil ways and escape God's judgment? Don't make the mistake of thinking, 'I can trace my family line back to Abraham, so I will be all right!' What God wants to see is good fruit from your lives. He wants to cut out the dead and rotten wood from the tree and throw it on the fire. He has sharpened his axe ready to make a start.

"Come now, speak out your sins and be baptized. Turn away from evil and do good. God's Promised One is coming very soon. He will sift out the good from the evil. Just like at harvest-time, he will gather up the good corn to store in his barns, but the dry, empty husks will go on the fire."

Some stood there fidgeting uncomfortably. They were not used to hearing talk like this. But then, miraculously, one or two of them stepped forward. Bravely, in front of all their fellows, they went down into the water and were baptized. Most of them, however, remained unmoved.

CHAPTER 11

God's Lamb

Day after day John preached. Hundreds of people flocked to hear him and be baptized. They then began to wait expectantly for God's special Messiah to appear.

John knew from his parents that Jesus had been born just six months after him. He knew that Jesus was living in Nazareth and working as a carpenter, but he didn't really know what to expect. In fact, he didn't even know what Jesus looked like. The only thing God had made clear to him was that one day he would see the Holy Spirit come down and settle on someone. By that sign, he would know for sure that this was the One. This man would be God's promised Messiah.

In the meantime, John knew that he had an important job to do. He had to prepare the people's hearts to receive their Heavenly King.

Late one afternoon, after John had been preaching and baptizing all day, it was time for the people to make their way home before it got dark. He was sitting beside the river, drying his feet and putting his sandals on, when a man came and sat alongside him.

"John," he said, "I can see that you have had a busy day, but there is one more job to be done."

"Oh yes?" replied John, concentrating on fastening his sandals.

"I want you to baptize me before you leave the river."

John knew from his accent that this man was from Galilee. He turned to him, and their eyes met. He knew that he should know this man, but he couldn't place him.

"It's Jesus from Nazareth in Galilee," said the man, reaching out his hand.

John felt a strange rise of excitement from deep inside. He had a sense that he had experienced this feeling before, but he couldn't remember when.

"Jesus. My own dear kinsman," said John, clutching his hand warmly. "I have been waiting for this pleasure." Both men stood and embraced.

Then Jesus gripped John by the shoulders. He held him at arms' length and looked earnestly at him.

"I'm serious, John. I want you to baptize me."

"B-but this cannot be. It would be madness," replied John, with a troubled look on his face. "I cannot baptize you. It's you who should be baptizing me."

"No," said Jesus. "It is important that we do it like this. I know that my Father wants it so."

John reluctantly agreed. He took off his sandals again, and the two men waded into the river. They stood there for a while. Jesus was quietly praying. John didn't quite know what to do.

"All right, John. I'm ready," Jesus said at last. "Take me down into the water."

John obeyed. He laid him back and let the water close over him, then he helped him to his feet. Jesus stood there with the water dripping from him, his head bowed. He was praying, so John just stood quietly next to him.

All of a sudden, the sky around them seemed to tear apart. Jesus remained unmoved, his head bowed, but John looked up at the sky. There it was, bright and clear, the likeness of a dove, coming down upon Jesus. This was the sign that John had been waiting for. He took a few steps backwards. Then he heard the voice. It seemed to come from the air all around them.

"This is my dearly loved Son. I am so pleased with him."

Both men stood in the water in silence for a while. Jesus, with head bowed, knew that the important task for which he had come was about to begin. John, looking on, realized that his own job would soon be coming to an end. He knew that this man from Nazareth must become greater. His reputation would grow. The crowds would begin to gather around him. John knew that many of the people who had flocked to hear him and be baptized in the Jordan would now begin to turn away and follow this man Jesus. It was God's plan. Now John must step back into the shadows and let Jesus have the limelight.

"He must grow greater," he said to himself. "I must become less."

The two men waded together up out of the river, both of them deep in thought.

Jesus knew that the Holy Spirit had come upon him, ready for the work that was ahead. He knew that he would not be going back to his carpenter's bench in Nazareth. Something new had begun, here in the Jordan river.

As Jesus left and went on his way, John knew that this short chapter in his life was coming to an end. He didn't know what would happen next. He continued to preach in and around the Jordan. Crowds of people still came to hear him and be baptized, even people from Samaria, whom the Jewish people considered to be second-class citizens. But John knew that this work he was doing would not last much longer.

Some weeks later, Jesus visited again. When John saw him, he said to those around him, "Look, here is God's Lamb. He will take away the sins of the world."

Some of John's own disciples, who had supported him in his work, decided to leave him and follow Jesus. Among them were some of the fishermen from Galilee.

John knew that this was good and right for them, but it was hard for him to let them go. It was another reminder that this work of preparing the way for Jesus was coming to an end. But there was worse to come.

CHAPTER 12

Herod Antipas

Herod Antipas lived in Tiberius on the shores of Lake Galilee, but he also had a stronghold on the far side of the Dead Sea. It was called Machaerus. There he had a palace, with luxurious rooms, where he could live in comfort with his wife and where he could entertain important guests.

Beneath this opulence were the dungeons, built into the hard rock and fitted with heavy iron doors. These dungeons were anything but comfortable and luxurious. Here, cruel Herod kept anyone who had offended him, or that he simply didn't like.

Herod Antipas was a nasty man, who came from an even nastier family. His father was called Herod the Great, who was most famous for killing all the children after the visit of the Wise Men. A better name for him would be "Herod the not-so-great".

Herod Antipas, together with a bunch of soldiers, regularly journeyed on horseback between Tiberius, Machaerus, and Jerusalem. This meant that they were often riding along the Jordan valley and crossing the river at the ford. So, from time to time, Herod and his men would come across John when he was preaching and baptizing.

Herod had done a lot of evil things, including stealing the wife of his half-brother Philip. She was called Herodias, and she had a daughter called Salome.

Herod had to admit that John was a very good preacher. It was quite entertaining to listen to him, and to watch all sorts of people going down into the water to speak out their mistakes and be baptized. John had often caught sight of Herod and his men as they went by. He had noticed that sometimes they would stop and watch what was going on.

Herod knew that there were many things in his life that were wrong. He wished that he could do what these people were doing, but he knew that it would never be possible. The list was too long. It would make him look weak, and he would risk losing the respect of the people. Nevertheless, he was fascinated by it all. He respected John and loved to hear him preach.

One day, when he was on his travels, Herod came across John at a quiet moment. There were not as many people about as usual. He told the soldiers to stop. He jumped down from his horse and gave the reins to one of his bodyguards.

"Stay here," he said to his men. "I want to talk with this fellow." He strode purposefully over to John.

"I need to speak with you," he said to John, "in private." As he said these words, he signalled that he wanted to be at a distance from his soldiers and the few people who were nearby. He didn't want anyone to overhear this conversation.

The two men turned and walked away along the riverbank. Then, after a few paces, John turned to face Herod. John remembered how Elijah had stood up to Ahab and his wicked wife Jezebel all those years ago. It gave him courage. John could see Herod for who he was – just an ordinary man, but with a huge burden of guilt and a conscience that had become twisted over the years. He felt compassion for him and longed to see him set free from the evil that had troubled him all his life.

How wonderful it would be, he thought, *if this man could speak out his sins and turn to follow God's holy ways.*

Although Herod was a powerful man, he had a strange fear of John. He knew that he was a holy man who did what was right. He knew that John was not afraid of him, as most people were. John looked him straight in the eye and spoke the truth clearly and boldly.

"Well Sir," John spoke politely, "what can I do for you?"

"John, err, now let's say…" began Herod hesitantly. "Let's say, err, for example, that I wanted to be baptized. What would you want me to do?"

The people watched as these two unlikely men talked together: the one, long-haired and roughly dressed, but totally still and calm; the other, clean-shaven and smartly dressed, but fidgeting uncomfortably.

The people looked at one another. They were all thinking the same thing: *This could go badly wrong*.

John took a deep breath. There was a lot to explain.

"All the people in this land and right across the world are suffering from the same sickness. We have sinned, turned our backs on God's holy laws. We have all gone astray, like a flock of sheep, as our great prophet Isaiah has said, but God has sent his promised Messiah, who will take away that sin once and for all. My job is to prepare the people for his coming. Many hundreds of people have come down here to the Jordan to speak out their sins and be baptized, so that they will be ready for him when he appears."

"So, what about me, John?" asked Herod earnestly. "You can't expect me to do that."

"There are things going on in your life, Sir, that are against God's laws. You could make a start by putting them right."

"What do you know about my life?" asked Herod defensively.

"Not much, Sir, but everybody knows that the woman you have married is your niece, and the wife of your brother Philip." John looked Herod straight in the eye. "What you have done is against God's Law. You know that, don't you, Sir?"

There was a long silence. Herod stared at the ground. He kicked a small stone and sent it bouncing down the bank and into the water.

"Hmm," he said at last. "We will speak more about this another time perhaps, but not now. I must be on my way."

He turned and walked briskly back to his men. He mounted his horse and rode swiftly away without saying a word. His soldiers followed him.

Thoughtfully, John watched him go. He had a feeling that one day Herod would meet Jesus, the carpenter from Nazareth.

CHAPTER 13

Herodias

Herod the Great had killed three of his own sons, one of his wives, and many members of that wife's family. Then he had sent his soldiers to kill all the young boys in and around Jerusalem, just because he had heard from the Wise Men that they thought a new king might have been born in the area.

Herod Antipas was one of Herod the Great's sons. Like his father, he was cruel and murderous. He cared little for God's laws. He had divorced his wife Aritas so that he could marry Herodias. She was the daughter of one of his half-brothers, and wife of another half-brother called Philip.

For Herodias, being married to someone like Herod Antipas was a tricky business. She knew that if she fell out with him, anything could happen, but she had grown up in the Herod family, so she knew how to get things done. After all, Herod the Great was her grandfather.

Herodias was cunning. She always wanted to have things her own way and didn't like anybody telling her what to do.

When she heard from Antipas what John had said about their marriage, she was very angry. In true Herod-family style, she thought that the only real answer was to kill John. It did not occur to her that she might have done something wrong herself. It was John that would have to go. Then everything would be all right again.

Herodias started to work out how she might get rid of John, but she did not let her husband see that she was upset. That would spoil things. She would wait. She knew that, sooner or later, an opportunity would arise for her to have him killed.

Herodias knew that John was very popular. She had heard about the crowds that were flocking to hear him. She would have to come up with a clever plan.

One evening, when she and her husband Antipas were alone together, she made her first move.

"Antipas, darling," she began, snuggling up close to him. "It has been months since you took me out in the chariot. Your public will be getting worried about me."

"All right, my dear," responded Antipas with a chuckle. "Where would you like to go?"

"Do you think you could take me to hear that preacher John? Everybody is talking about him."

"Steady on," said Antipas. "He might persuade you to be baptized in the Jordan river and confess your sins. Then where would we be?"

"Don't be silly, my darling. I just want to see what all the fuss is about. Nobody is going to get me into the Jordan."

"Don't you be so sure," said Antipas. "He's a very persuasive preacher."

"Even the servants have been to hear John," said Herodias sulkily. "Sometimes it feels as though I am out of touch. Whoever heard of a queen who knows less than her servants?" So it went on, until Herod agreed to take her.

Early one morning, two of the best horses were harnessed to the four-wheeler. A posse of horsemen accompanied them, and they set off along the Jordan valley in search of John. He was not difficult to find.

It was nearly midday when Herod's chariot reached the spot where John was at work preaching and baptizing. There were people everywhere. Herod and his party were able to stop in the shade of some trees. They watched the goings-on out of sight, well behind the crowd.

John was in full flow, preaching from the riverbank. They could hear every word.

"If any one of you has two coats, that's one too many. Give one away. Give it to the poor fellow who has none."

75

"These are dangerous words," whispered Herodias to her husband, "and so many people are listening!"

"I told you that he is a powerful preacher." Herod kept his voice down, so that he would not be overheard.

"But all these people," repeated Herodias. "What do the Romans think of it all?"

"I don't know," answered Herod with a shrug. I don't suppose they are too worried. In fact, the troops tell me that some of them have been to hear John. Some have even been baptized by him." This news came as a shock to Herodias, but John's voice reverberated through the valley.

"Some of you have asked me if I am God's promised Messiah. No, I tell you. I am not the Christ. One is coming after me who is much more powerful. I am simply that voice calling in the wilderness, of which the prophet Isaiah has written." Here John spoke with such passion that few could resist him.

"Make the road straight and smooth for him. Those crooked paths – get them straightened out. Those rough ways, make them smooth, and we will see God's mighty salvation come upon us all."

The crowd clapped and cheered. Herodias heard these words too. She knew what the cost would be for her to straighten things out in her life. No, never! She could sense God speaking to her and challenging her. It made her feel very uncomfortable, but she resolved not to give in.

This man has got to go, she thought. She leaned across to Antipas and took his hand.

"You have got to do something," she said. "You cannot let this sort of thing carry on. You will end up in trouble with Caesar."

"You could be right, my dear," answered Herod. "But these are fine words. I really admire this man."

"He makes me shudder," replied Herodias. "If you had any sense, Antipas, you would lock him up, before we have a riot on our hands. I think we ought to go," she continued. "I don't feel very well. Please take me home." She gripped his hand tightly and he gave the order to his driver to take them back along the Jordan valley to Tiberius.

They journeyed back in silence, each of them deep in their own thoughts. Antipas was considering what his wife had said. Would John's preaching lead to unrest among the people of the region for which he was responsible? What would happen if he put John in prison? With so many people flocking to hear him, that alone could lead to a riot. What if John was right, and there was another, more powerful, preacher on the way? What would happen then?

Herodias was planning her next move. She had one simple goal in her mind – to get John killed. The question was how, but she felt that today she had made good progress. If she could just persuade Herod to lock John up, that would be another step in the right direction.

CHAPTER 14

Prison

When John heard from those who had seen them that Herod and his wife had been at the Jordan that day, he guessed that he would not have many days left to preach to the crowd and point them to Jesus.

Each day, his voice seemed to grow stronger, his words more urgent. He wanted to persuade as many people as possible to turn away from him, John, and go in search of Jesus.

It was during this time that some of his disciples came and spoke to him. They were really upset.

"You know that man you were telling us about, the one you called 'God's Lamb'? Well, he is baptizing people now. He can't do that, surely? That's your job."

"I can only do what God has given me to do," replied John. "I am like a bridegroom's friend at a wedding, who has to step aside at the last minute. I am full of joy to hear this news about Jesus. I know that my job will soon be over. He must get greater and more important. I must step back and become less and less."

It was only a matter of weeks after this that, early one morning, when John arrived at the river to begin his preaching, he was greeted by a group of soldiers on horseback. As soon as he saw that they had a spare horse with them, all saddled up, he knew that they had come to take him away. He had been expecting something like this.

The leader of the group dismounted and gave the reins to one of the other horsemen. He came to meet John.

"Good morning, John," he began. John sensed that he felt a bit awkward about what they had come to do. "We are under orders to take you to Herod."

"I thought it might come to this," answered John. "I will come, but I am not accustomed to being on horseback, you know."

"It's a long way," replied the soldier. "We are taking you to Machaerus."

The soldiers helped John onto his horse. They all set off across the river and then south, towards the Dead Sea. It was a strange sight: the soldiers in their smart and polished uniforms, and then John with his bushy beard and long hair blowing in the wind, his rough camel-hair coat strapped at the waist with a leather belt.

One or two early arrivals at the river had seen John go, so word soon got around that he had been arrested and taken away. It wasn't long before Jesus heard the news. This was the signal for him. It was time to begin his public work in Galilee.

The soldiers treated John with respect. He was one of the most revered men in Judaea, and some of these soldiers had family members who had heard John preach.

They rode most of that day, stopping from time to time to rest the horses and to let John stretch his legs.

Overnight, they stayed at an inn. John wanted to sleep under a bush somewhere; it was more his style. But the soldiers insisted that he must have a room. They did not want to lose him.

Late the following morning, they arrived at Herod's heavily guarded stronghold. Machaerus was an imposing place, built on a steep-sided mountain of rock. Herod's luxurious rooms were at the top, complete with a banqueting hall and even a Roman bath in the latest style. There was also a tall stone look-out tower with a commanding view of the surrounding country.

There was a wide range of accommodation. On the one hand were Herod's five-star state rooms, then there were the more modest servants' quarters, then rough-and-ready billets for the soldiers. Finally, there were the dungeons hewn out of the solid rock, with great iron doors that squeaked open, and closed with a loud echoing clang.

John's accommodation was not at the luxury end of things. His room was more like a cave. He didn't really mind this too much. He was used to living in the desert and sleeping in caves. Many people among Herod's staff and soldiers at Machaerus knew John and greatly respected him as a courageous and godly man, so he was well looked after.

Herod, too, admired and respected John. From time to time, he would have John cleaned up and brought up to his royal apartments, so that he could talk with him.

John was not fooled by the lavish furnishings or the size of the defending walls. He could see that this man was full of fear. The whole fortress palace was a clear sign to John that Herod Antipas lived with the constant worry that his enemies would attack him, or that jealous members of his family would plot against him.

John knew that the whole business of Herod's divorce from his previous wife and his marriage to Herodias had ruffled some feathers. Consequently, he had some powerful enemies.

Herod was intrigued by John. He knew no one else like him. John would look him in the eye and speak directly into his life. It fascinated and challenged him, but he was too much of a coward to face the evil that he himself had done. He wasn't brave enough to put anything right.

Herod had a feeling that John wanted him to confess all his sins and then be baptized. He had seen him eyeing up his fashionable Roman bath.

"He's not going to baptize me in there, if that's what he thinks," he said to himself. "What would become of me?"

Little did Herod know that, because of his cowardice and ever-present fear, and because he wasn't brave enough to sort out this business with Herodias, John would soon be gone. Herod would have to run for his life into exile, pursued by the father of the wife that he had turned out of his palace.

CHAPTER 15

Doubts

For John, the discomfort of prison didn't bother him too much. He was used to hardship, and he enjoyed the opportunities that he had daily, to talk with the soldiers and prison guards. He also had occasional visits from the men and women who had helped him during his time preaching and baptizing.

It was from these disciples of his that he was able to hear snippets of news about Jesus, though Galilee was a long way from Herod's stronghold at Machaerus.

During the long, dark nights, and other times when he was alone, John was troubled by occasional doubts.

Did I get it right? he wondered. *Is Jesus really the One?*

As these prison days turned into weeks, and then months, the occasional doubts became nagging worries. John became increasingly restless, pacing to and fro in his cell. He longed to be able to get out and walk all the way to Galilee and see for himself.

"What if I was wrong, Lord?" he prayed. "Have I wasted all these years? I really need to know. There must be a way."

The next time he had a visit from a couple of his disciples, they could see that he wasn't his usual peaceful self. They stood outside the iron gate to his cell under the watchful eye of the prison guard.

"We've brought you a treat, John – a lovely piece of honeycomb."

"Thanks," said John, taking the jar of honeycomb through the bars. "Thank you so much." But there was not the usual enthusiasm in his voice. He sounded tired and sad, and a bit distant.

"What is the matter?" they asked. "You seem troubled."

"I am, my brothers. I am troubled," he answered. "I've been thinking. What if I have got it wrong? What if Jesus from Nazareth is not really God's Messiah? What then?" John gripped the bars until his knuckles showed white. He stared earnestly at his friends. "What then, eh?"

There was a long and awkward silence. Then one of them spoke.

"Would you like us to go and speak to him, John? Would that help, do you think?"

"Yes, it would. I would go myself, but look at me. I am not sure that I will ever get out of this place. There are not many that do."

"Don't speak like this! You have done a great job. Everybody knows you have. We will go and find Jesus, and we will ask him straight, 'Are you God's Messiah?'"

"That's so good of you, my friends. Ask him from me, 'Are you the one who is to come, or should we wait for another?' Let's hear what he has to say. I will wait for you to bring me his reply."

It was a long journey from Herod's fortress all the way up to Galilee in the north, where Jesus was at work. There would be a long wait before John saw his friends again.

John knew the Scriptures well. Much of them he had learned by heart. He knew that when God's Promised One came, there would be some extraordinary goings-on. The blind would be able to see. Lame people would walk. Deaf people would be able to hear. All sorts of amazing things would take place.

All this would be really good news for everyone, but particularly for poor people, who could never afford to see a doctor, and were not normally able to help themselves when things in life went wrong.

As he waited, John had a lot of time to think. He would sometimes daydream about his boyhood. He fondly remembered visiting Jerusalem with his parents, going to the Temple with his father, or watching his mother haggling with the traders in the busy streets.

It cheered him to recall these scenes. He remembered the journeys across the rugged wilderness of the Judaean desert, and his father showing him how to take honey from a wild bees' nest without getting stung. He remembered making simple meals over a small fire of thorn twigs. He even learned how to catch and cook locusts and grasshoppers. They were delicious.

These were happy memories, but he realized how God was preparing him for the years that lay ahead. He thanked God for his dear and faithful parents, who had taught him so well. He was thankful too for the monastery, for the welcome that was always there, for the library where he could study the Scriptures, and for the wisdom, learning, and encouragement of the brothers.

John understood that this was training for his work of preaching and baptizing. He wanted to be sure that after all this wonderful preparation, he hadn't made a serious mistake and failed in the task that God had given him to do.

Sometimes he would lie awake at night in his cell, with these doubtful thoughts going round and round in his mind. Then he would remember the day when Jesus had visited him at the Jordan river, when the voice came from heaven, and he saw that strange bright dove-shaped presence coming down and resting upon Jesus.

"Yes, he must have been the right man. I did get it right, Lord. I have completed the work that you asked me to do."

With these comforting memories in his heart, he would turn over on his straw mattress and try to sleep again. Then, a few nights later, the old anxiety would creep back into his thoughts, and he would lie awake once more, turning it all over again in his mind, until at last, one day, his friends returned with news of Jesus.

It was getting late in the afternoon when they arrived. They had been walking for days and were hot and tired. John was so pleased to see them again.

"I am sorry, my friends, that I cannot wash your feet or give you water. This is an inhospitable place, and these iron bars get in the way."

"Don't worry, John. It is enough to see you again and bring you news."

"How did you get on?" asked John anxiously. "Did you speak with Jesus?"

"Yes, we did," they replied, "and we asked him your question."

"And?" asked John, staring intently at them through the bars.

"He told us to tell you what we saw and heard, and it is all truly amazing. You have made no mistakes, John. He is the One. There is no doubt. Blind people are seeing. Lame people are walking. People with leprosy are being made completely clean. Deaf people are hearing; even some dead people have been brought back to life. So many ordinary poor people are being blessed."

John was listening to this news with his eyes closed. His face was turned upwards, and he was smiling. The tears were rolling down his face, and then losing their way in his tangled beard.

"Then he said some words that were especially for you, John," they continued. "He said, 'Blessed is the man who does not lose heart because of me.'"

John stood in silence for a while, gripping the bars. His eyes remained closed.

The guard was the next to speak.

"Your time is up you two," he said gruffly, but not unkindly. "You need to be on your way well before nightfall. There's nothing for miles from here."

John opened his eyes and looked directly at these two faithful friends. He reached through the bars and took their hands. His eyes were wet with tears, but his face was shining with joy.

"Thank you. Thank you, my dear friends. What you have told me has brought great comfort."

As John's disciples said goodbye to him and set out upon their long walk back to Judaea, they also felt comforted that their trip to Galilee and back had brought John the reassurance that his work had not been in vain. Now he would be able to sleep peacefully at night. He would no longer be troubled by the anxious thoughts that kept him awake.

John felt so warmed by the visit of these dear faithful disciples of his. They had understood his concerns and gone to such great lengths to put his mind at rest.

So, Jesus was the One whom God had promised. There was no doubt at all. It was all as foretold by the prophet. Now John could rest assured that he had fulfilled the purpose for which he had come. He had completed the task that God had prepared him for.

John felt a new lightness come over him. He slept soundly at night, and he spent his days reciting the words of the prophets and singing the psalms, which he knew by heart.

Strangely, he found himself singing the pilgrim psalms, which the Jewish people sang when they were heading towards the Holy City for the festivals. He felt a growing excitement, just as he had as a boy when his family were preparing for a festival holiday.

CHAPTER 16

Home at Last

Lots of people were arriving at Herod's stronghold. John could hear the chariot wheels on the gravel and people talking and laughing. He knew that something was going on. He asked the prison guard about it, who told him that it was Herod's birthday.

"There are posh people coming from all over," he told John. "There will be feasting and drinking and dancing, but I don't suppose it will make much difference to us, John. We will get the same rations as usual."

"They can keep their wine," replied John. "I have never touched a drop of the stuff. I was set apart to serve God from the day I was born. No alcohol. No haircuts. That was all part of the deal, and I don't regret it for one moment. God has been so faithful."

People kept arriving all that day, and the noise from the state rooms high up in the fortress got louder and louder. As darkness began to fall, the music started.

John pictured the scene. He had visited Herod many times in his fancy rooms. He knew that Herod and Herodias would be welcoming their guests. All the lamps would be burning, their flames sparkling in the polished tableware. The tables would be loaded with bread and fruit and all sorts of delicacies, while servant girls went to and fro among the guests with jugs of wine, to make sure that everyone had plenty to drink.

As the evening wore on, the guests got noisier. The music grew louder and more rhythmic. John could hear that the guests were dancing, and as time went by, everything got more and more wild. He could hear the clapping and the stamping feet. He could hear the squeals and giggles of the women, the coarse laughter and rude shouts of the men.

Then, all of a sudden, the music stopped and everything went quiet. John thought that the party was coming to an end, so he settled down on his mattress, pulled the blanket over him, and tried to get some sleep.

Before he could nod off, the music started again, but this was a very different tune. It was slow and sensuous. It reminded him of the snakes that he had often watched in the desert, slithering their way along in the sand towards their prey.

This strange music got louder and faster and wilder. People started clapping in time to the hypnotic rhythm. John could hear the men calling out coarse comments in drunken voices. It gave him the creeps.

John remembered the story of Belshazzar's feast, when the evil king of Babylon called for the sacred cups that had been captured from the Temple in Jerusalem. Everybody had been noisily dancing, feasting, and drinking wine from the sacred cups, when suddenly all went quiet, and Belshazzar's face turned as white as a sheet. There, up on the wall of the banqueting hall, a man's hand had appeared. It was writing some mysterious words that nobody could understand. God was sending the king a serious message.

John turned over in his cold, dark cell. Strangely enough, all had gone quiet in the rooms above him. He settled down again and tried to sleep, but then he heard the heavy tread of the prison guard and the jangle of keys.

"John," called the guard gruffly, "you're wanted."

John looked up. In the flickering light of the guard's torch, he could see an anxious expression on the face of his guard.

"What's happened?" asked John, getting up from his bed. "Is everything all right? You look troubled."

"I am, John. I hate these parties. Anything can happen when that lot get drunk."

"I know what you mean," replied John. "Things can get out of control."

"They want your head, John," blurted out the guard, as he wiped away a tear.

"Don't let it trouble you, my friend," replied John, placing a comforting hand on the guard's shoulder. "They can have it. I don't need it anymore. I am going on a journey. There is a bit of honeycomb in the pot. Take it home for your wife."

The guard solemnly led John out into the prison yard. More soldiers were there with torches. A great axe with a curved blade stood against the wall. Its sharp, bright edge glinted in the torchlight.

John knelt by the big wooden block. He was entirely at peace in his heart. He knew that he had completed the mission that God had made him for. He thought of Elijah, and how God's special chariot had come to whisk him away.

He felt the prison guard lift his long hair out of the way of the axe. There was a flash of brightness as the sharp blade fell, and he was free, striding out upon the road towards the beautiful city. A great, overwhelming joy filled his heart. An ancient song was on his lips as he marched along.

"Give thanks to the Lord,
For He is good.
His love endures for ever."

He passed through the shining gates and into

the city. Trumpets heralded his arrival. Crowds of people lined the streets, all clapping and cheering him home.

Coming towards him was a man he recognized. He was carrying before him in both hands a sparkling crown of gold. It was Jesus himself.

"This is for you, John," he said, placing it on his head. "It is the martyr's crown. You have been faithful, my dear friend, even to the point of death." The air resounded with shouts of joy.

It didn't seem strange to John that Jesus should be here, nor when Elizabeth and Zechariah came to greet him, that they were surrounded by so many beautiful children.

John knew deep inside that this place was subject to a heavenly order. Time and space worked differently here. The whole shining city was filled with a different kind of light. This was the home that he had been longing for. This was where he truly belonged.

Best of all, this was the place where Jesus the Lamb was King!

ALSO AVAILABLE

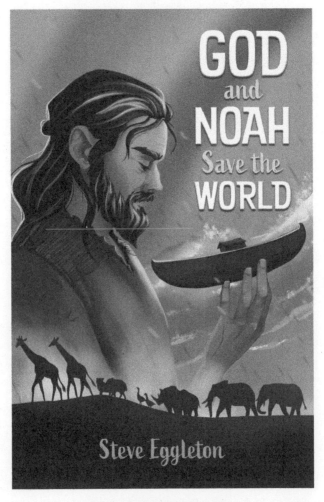

ISBN: 978 0 7459 7877 2